A Bigg

Written by
Stephen Rickard

Illustrated by
Tom Heard

Jeevan is sitting near the river.
He is sitting in the summer sun.

It is hot. It is too hot for Jeevan.

Jeevan sees a big red banner.
This banner will keep a bit of sun off him.

Jeevan sits near the banner.
Yes, that is a bit better.
Jeevan is a bit cooler now.

Then Jeevan sees a bigger banner.

Is the bigger banner better for Jeevan?

Yes, Jeevan is sure that the bigger banner is better. It will keep off all of the sun.

Jeevan will be much cooler.

But Jeevan needs to check that the bigger banner is secure.

If it is not secure, it might tip onto him. Then Jeevan might get hurt.

Jeevan is sure that the banner is secure. Now he can chill in the sun.

Jeevan looks in the river.
It looks cool.

Jeevan has a wish: can he be in the cool river?

Then Jeevan sees a fish in the river.
It is not a big fish.

Jeevan looks at the fish.

If he had a net, he might get the fish for dinner.

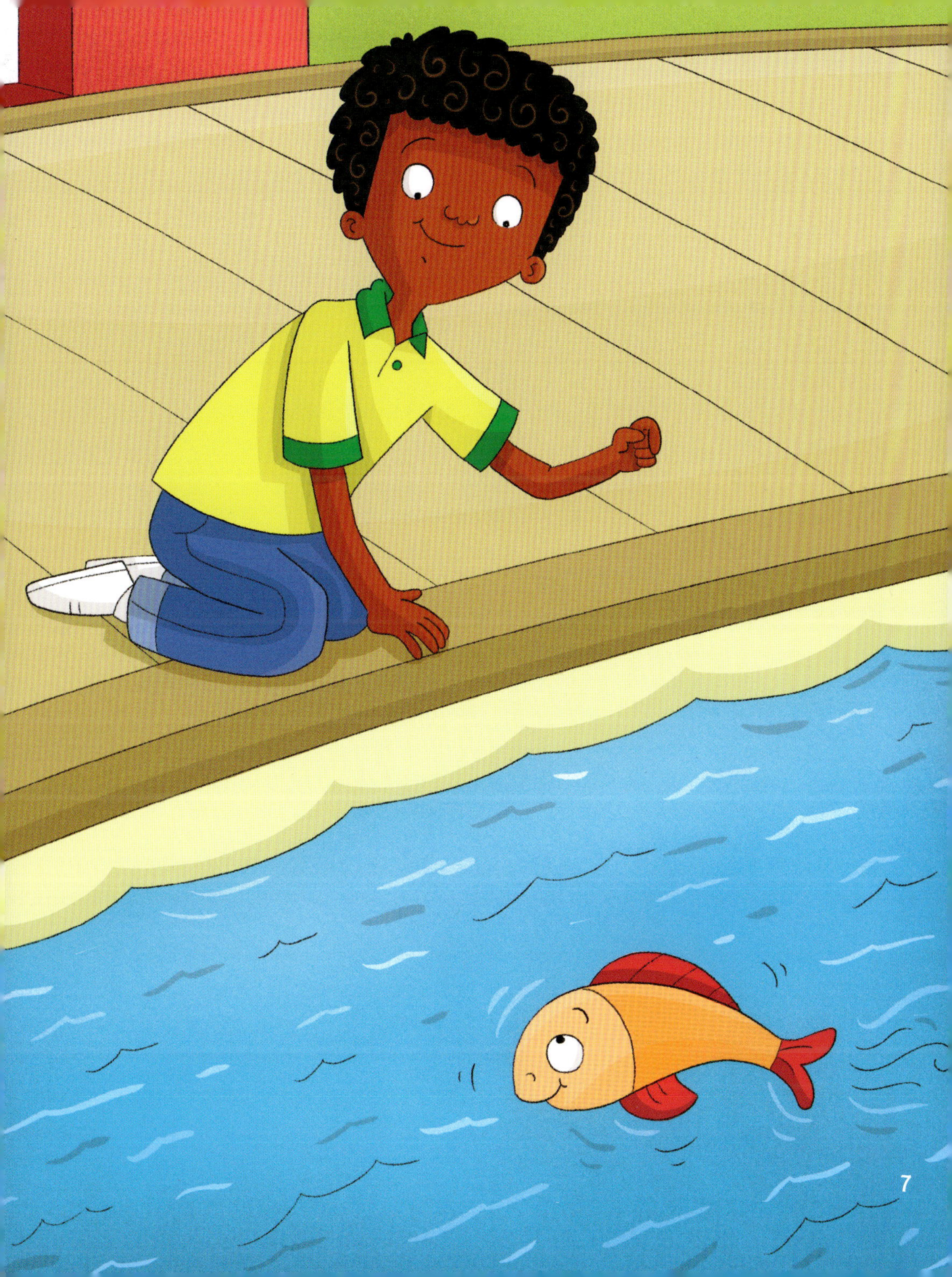

Then Jeevan sees a bigger fish in the river.

Jeevan is sure that this fish is bigger and longer.

Jeevan will get the bigger fish for dinner.

But he is not sure. Will he cook the fish for dinner, or for supper?

The river is pure. He is sure that the fish will be good to cook.

Jeevan gets a fishing net.
Can he get the fish?

But look! The banner is not secure.
It tips onto Jeevan.

Now Jeevan is in the river.
He is wet.

The fish cannot be seen.

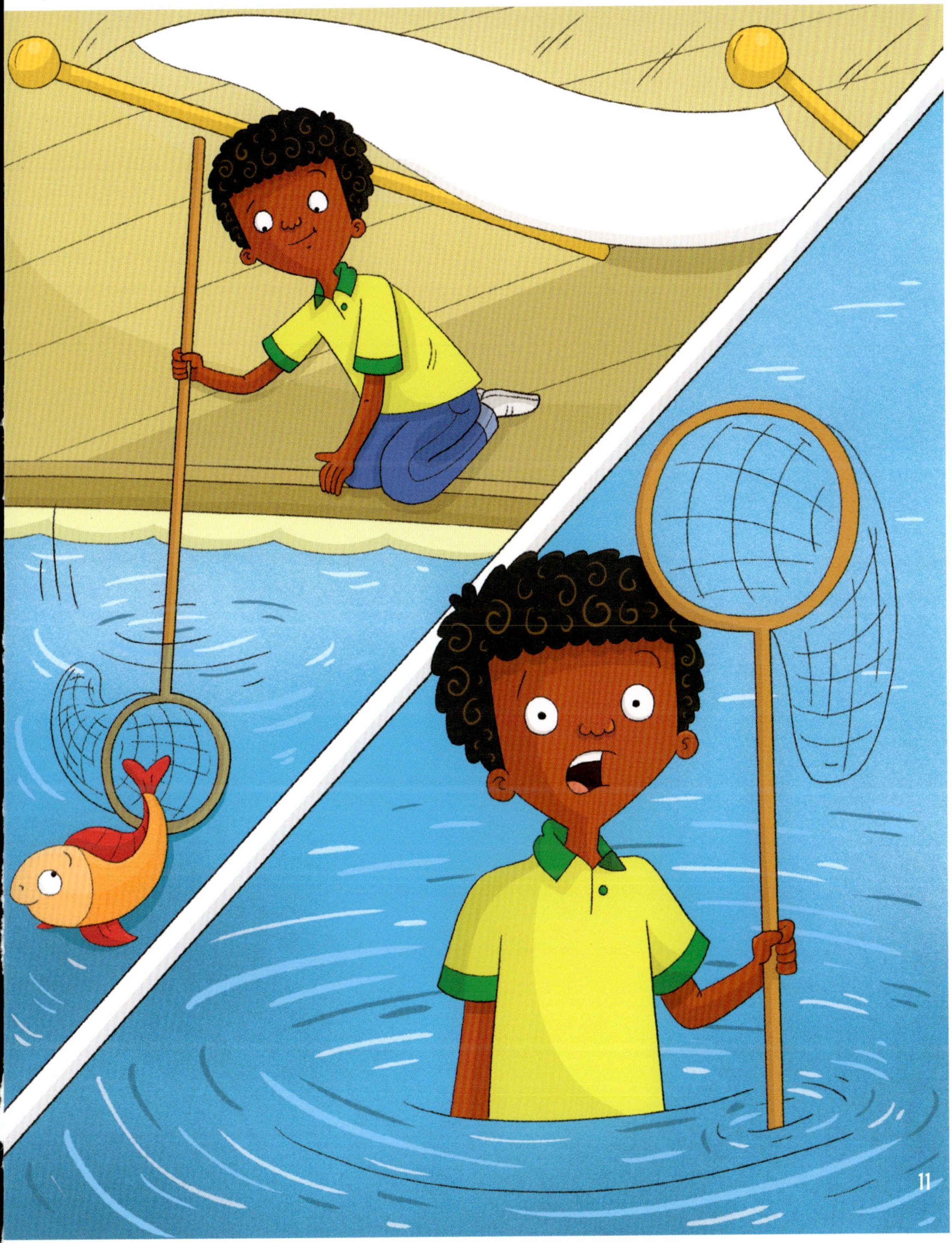

Jeevan has no fish for supper, but now he is not as hot!

This was his wish.
Now he is cool in the river!